TROMBONE / EUPHONIUM BC/TC / BASSOON

Messiah at CHRISTMAS

GEORGE FREDERIC HANDEL

Arranged by James Curnow (ASCAP)

CURNOW® MUSIC

Order Number: CMP 1179-06-400

George Frederic Handel
Arranged by James Curnow (ASCAP)
MESSIAH AT CHRISTMAS
Trombone / Euphonium BC/TC / Bassoon

ISBN-10: 90-431-2596-2
ISBN-13: 978-90-431-2596-3

CD number: 19-089-3 CMP

GEORGE FREDERIC HANDEL

Arranged by James Curnow

Christmas Greetings!

Music at Christmas is an extremely important part of celebrating this most wonderful time of year. As we celebrate the birth of our Lord Jesus Christ, music adds much joy to the celebration.

George Frederic Handel (1685-1759) composed the entire Messiah (based on scriptural passages as arranged by Jennes) in only twenty-four days. The Christmas part of this work is generally most familiar, and more often performed, and contains a wealth of important arias and choruses that can have a tremendous impact on worship during the Christmas season.

The ten arrangements in this collection are designed to allow average to advanced players the opportunity to perform in church, school, in public or anywhere Christmas is being celebrated. As you will note, I have not used the arias and choruses in their entirety, so that their duration will better fit into a worship setting, but all of the pieces have been carefully arranged to include the original melodic content. Please refer to the scriptural references for each piece (see Contents page) during your preparation and performance of the music, as this will help you to better understand Handel's intent in creating his masterpiece of Christmas worship.

Each solo book includes an accompaniment CD which contains a sample performance of each solo, as well as the accompaniment only. This will allow the performer to practice with the accompaniment when an accompanist is not available. The accompaniment track can also be used for performances if desired. Appropriate tuning notes have been added to the compact disc recording to allow the soloist the opportunity to adjust their intonation to the intonation of the compact disc accompaniment. A separate piano accompaniment book is available.

I hope you will enjoy this addition to your Christmas celebration repertoire.

James Curnow
Composer/arranger

Contents

◯ Solo with accompaniment

⬤ Accompaniment

1. COMFORT YE

G.F. Handel

from "Messiah"

Arr. by **James Curnow** (ASCAP)

G.F. Handel
2. EV'RY VALLEY SHALL BE EXALTED
from "Messiah"

Arr. by **James Curnow** (ASCAP)

Track
5 **6**

G.F. Handel
3. AND THE GLORY OF THE LORD
from "Messiah"

Arr. by **James Curnow** (ASCAP)

G.F. Handel
4. BUT WHO MAY ABIDE THE DAY OF HIS COMING
from "Messiah"

Arr. by **James Curnow** (ASCAP)

5. O THOU THAT TELLEST GOOD TIDINGS TO ZION

G.F. Handel

from "Messiah"

Arr. by **James Curnow** (ASCAP)

G.F. Handel
6. FOR UNTO US A CHILD IS BORN
from "Messiah"
Arr. by **James Curnow** (ASCAP)

7. PASTORAL SYMPHONY

from "Messiah"

Arr. by **James Curnow** (ASCAP)

Track

Larghetto e mezzo piano (♩. = 44)

G.F. Handel

8. REJOICE GREATLY, O DAUGHTER OF ZION

from "Messiah"

Arr. by **James Curnow** (ASCAP)

Track

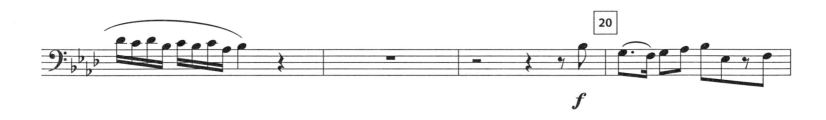

G.F. Handel
9. HE SHALL FEED HIS FLOCK LIKE A SHEPHERD
from "Messiah"

Arr. by **James Curnow** (ASCAP)

Track
⑲ ⑳

Larghetto e piano (♩. = 48)

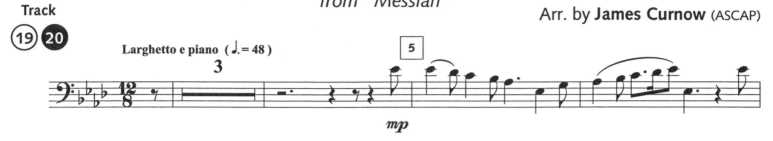

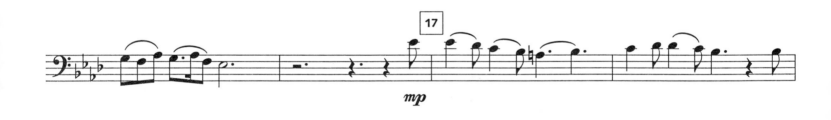

G.F. Handel

10. HALLELUJAH CHORUS

from "Messiah"

Arr. by **James Curnow** (ASCAP)

Track

G.F. Handel
1. COMFORT YE
from "Messiah"

Arr. by **James Curnow** (ASCAP)

2. EV'RY VALLEY SHALL BE EXALTED

from "Messiah"

Arr. by **James Curnow** (ASCAP)

Track

G.F. Handel

3. AND THE GLORY OF THE LORD

from "Messiah"

Arr. by **James Curnow** (ASCAP)

G.F. Handel

4. BUT WHO MAY ABIDE THE DAY OF HIS COMING

from "Messiah"

Arr. by **James Curnow** (ASCAP)

Track

G.F. Handel
5. O THOU THAT TELLEST GOOD TIDINGS TO ZION

from "Messiah"

Arr. by **James Curnow** (ASCAP)

G.F. Handel
6. FOR UNTO US A CHILD IS BORN
from "Messiah"

Arr. by **James Curnow** (ASCAP)

G.F. Handel
7. PASTORAL SYMPHONY
from "Messiah"

Arr. by **James Curnow** (ASCAP)

Track

Larghetto e mezzo piano (♩. = 44)

Rall.

G.F. Handel
8. REJOICE GREATLY, O DAUGHTER OF ZION
from "Messiah"

Arr. by **James Curnow** (ASCAP)

Track

G.F. Handel

9. HE SHALL FEED HIS FLOCK LIKE A SHEPHERD

from "Messiah"

Arr. by **James Curnow** (ASCAP)

Track

⑲ ⑳

Larghetto e piano (♩. = 48)

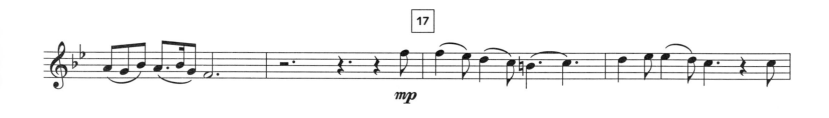

10. HALLELUJAH CHORUS

G.F. Handel

from "Messiah"

Arr. by **James Curnow** (ASCAP)

George Frederic Handel
Arranged by James Curnow (ASCAP)

MESSIAH AT EASTER

Music at Easter is an extremely important part of celebrating this wonderful time of year. As we celebrate the resurrection of our Lord Jesus Christ, music adds much joy to the celebration.

Though the Christmas part of the Messiah by Georg Frederic Handel is generally most familiar, and more often performed, the Easter portion contains a wealth of important arias and choruses that can have a tremendous impact on worship during the Easter season.

The ten arrangements in this collection are designed to allow average to advanced players the opportunity to perform in church, school, in public or anywhere Easter is being celebrated.

Each solo book includes an accompaniment CD which contains a sample performance of each solo, as well as the accompaniment only. This will allow the performer to practice with the accompaniment when an accompanist is not available. The accompaniment track can also be used for performances if desired. A separate piano accompaniment book is available.

1. Lift Up Your Heads
2. How Beautiful Are the Feet
3. Their Sound Has Gone Out
4. I Know That My Redeemer Liveth
5. Since By Man Came Death
6. The Trumpet Shall Sound
7. O Death Where Is Thy Sting and But Thanks Be To God
8. If God Before Us
9. Worthy Is The Lamb
10. Hallelujah Chorus

Flute / Oboe / Mallet Percussion	CMP 1184-06-400
Bb Clarinet	CMP 1185-06-400
Eb Alto Saxophone	CMP 1186-06-400
Bb Trumpet	CMP 1187-06-400
F Horn / Eb Horn	CMP 1188-06-400
Trombone / Euphonium BC/TC / Bassoon	CMP 1189-06-400
Piano / Organ Accompaniment	CMP 1190-06-400